A MUSIC TEACHER'S
Gratitude Journal

Creative Prompts to Nurture Joy, Reduce Stress, and Reflect on Your Teaching

By Krista Hart

alfred.com

Copyright © 2021 by Alfred Music
All rights reserved. Printed in USA.

ISBN-10: 1-4706-4740-0
ISBN-13: 978-1-4706-4740-7

Art resources courtesy of Getty Images

Introduction

All music teachers are deserving of self-care and creative space.

Think of all the events, big or small, in the day of a music teacher—everything from watching a "light bulb" moment happen for a student or the feeling of accomplishment found in your ensemble giving a flawless performance, to realizing you forgot to reserve the concert date on the school calendar or that a student dropped your class. How can you capitalize on those amazing moments and learn from the unfortunate ones? How do you cultivate a positive attitude? How do you maintain your personal passion for music? How do you stay inspired to do your job? There's no singular answer, but one tool that can help is a gratitude journal.

There have been many studies on the effects of practicing gratitude.

Some proven benefits include:

- Lower stress levels
- Increased mental strength and resilience
- Improved self-esteem
- Improved sleep
- Feeling healthier and experiencing fewer aches and pains

Who needs this journal?

- Anyone who is seeking to express appreciation and practice mindfulness
- Teachers who want to be and stay inspired
- Those who are looking for confidence in their career
- Musicians who want to activate their personal connection to music making
- Educators who strive to be at their very best for students in an authentic way

Each set of exercises includes a quote, a habit tracker, and five writing prompts leading you to express gratitude, reflect on your teaching, and ignite the joy of making music. Use the tracker to list habits you want to develop. Then fill in a circle each time you perform a habit. Every four weeks you will find instructions for "Song of Gratitude," a year-long guided composition project culminating in musically expressing your personal thankfulness and the opportunity to share it with others. These same step-by-step instructions can also be the basis for a songwriting project for your students.

Make this journal your own—you will not be graded on it! There are 36 sections so it can be completed as a weekly practice. There are five prompts in each section, so you might choose to complete one each day of the work week. Or, flip through the book and find a prompt that speaks to you on any particular day. The important thing is to set a practice routine and stick to it.

Change the wording of any prompt to better meet your needs. Replace "this week" with "today" or "this year," or substitute "class" for "student." Switch out any words that might not apply to your particular teaching situation.

Your responses can be as simple or involved as you feel necessary. Try not to judge your answers. You may find that you become more thoughtful and introspective the longer you use the journal.

Tips for getting the most out of your journaling experience:

- Set aside time to journal so that you can focus on it without distraction. Do your best not to rush through your responses.

- Keep your entries positive. Unlike a diary, you are not recording the day's events. Focusing on the good is part of what makes a gratitude journal unique.

- Challenge yourself to not repeat answers.

- Be creative—respond to a prompt with a poem, drawing, word cloud, or melody.

- It requires some discipline. Just like learning a new piece of music, it may not feel easy or sound good when you start, but before long it will feel more natural and become something you look forward to.

Yearly GOALS

Use this space to keep track of the things you dream of accomplishing this year. Keep yourself accountable by checking back each month to assess your progress.

_____

_____

_____

_____

_____

_____

_____

_____

_____

_____

_____

_____

_____

"*Gratitude* is the healthiest of all human emotions. The more you express gratitude for what you have, the more likely you will have even more to express gratitude for."

— ZIG ZIGLAR

HABIT TRACKER

HABIT	1	2	3	4	5	6	7
_____	○	○	○	○	○	○	○
_____	○	○	○	○	○	○	○
_____	○	○	○	○	○	○	○
_____	○	○	○	○	○	○	○
_____	○	○	○	○	○	○	○
_____	○	○	○	○	○	○	○
_____	○	○	○	○	○	○	○
_____	○	○	○	○	○	○	○
_____	○	○	○	○	○	○	○
_____	○	○	○	○	○	○	○
_____	○	○	○	○	○	○	○
_____	○	○	○	○	○	○	○

NOTES

....
....
....
....
....
....

🌿 _____

is a colleague that I can count on for

_____

_____

_____

_____

_____

🌿 List three words that define what you want to focus on this year.

1. ....

2. ....

3. ....

🌿 What did you learn this week that you are grateful for?

....

....

....

....

....

....

....

🎼 Musical Moment

What musical skills or abilities are you thankful to have? Why?

....

....

....

....

....

....

....

....

🎼 Teaching Reflection

What would your life be like if you weren't a music teacher?

....

....

....

....

....

....

....

....

"*Music Teacher* is a sacred profession. It's as sacred as it gets . . . You are now an important guidepost on the landscape of your students' lives forever."

— WYNTON MARSALIS

HABIT TRACKER

HABIT	1	2	3	4	5	6	7
_____	○	○	○	○	○	○	○
_____	○	○	○	○	○	○	○
_____	○	○	○	○	○	○	○
_____	○	○	○	○	○	○	○
_____	○	○	○	○	○	○	○
_____	○	○	○	○	○	○	○
_____	○	○	○	○	○	○	○
_____	○	○	○	○	○	○	○
_____	○	○	○	○	○	○	○
_____	○	○	○	○	○	○	○
_____	○	○	○	○	○	○	○
_____	○	○	○	○	○	○	○

NOTES

....
....
....
....
....
....

🪶 I am grateful to be a music teacher because

_____

_____

_____

_____

_____

_____

_____

_____

🪶 Illustrate the joy of making music.

🪶 Write about a person in your life that you're especially grateful for and why.

....

....

....

....

....

....

....

Musical Moment
What performances do you look forward to this year?

Teaching Reflection
What skills would you like to nurture that would help you be a better teacher?

"The *purpose* of life is to discover your gift. The *work* of life is to develop it. The *meaning* of life is to give your gift away."

— DAVID VISCOTT
FINDING YOUR STRENGTH IN DIFFICULT TIMES
McGraw-Hill

HABIT TRACKER

HABIT	1	2	3	4	5	6	7
_____	○	○	○	○	○	○	○
_____	○	○	○	○	○	○	○
_____	○	○	○	○	○	○	○
_____	○	○	○	○	○	○	○
_____	○	○	○	○	○	○	○
_____	○	○	○	○	○	○	○
_____	○	○	○	○	○	○	○
_____	○	○	○	○	○	○	○
_____	○	○	○	○	○	○	○
_____	○	○	○	○	○	○	○
_____	○	○	○	○	○	○	○
_____	○	○	○	○	○	○	○

NOTES

....
....
....
....
....
....

🪶 I am grateful for my ability to

_____

_____

because

_____

_____

_____

_____

_____

🪶 List three intangible benefits of your job.

1. ....

2. ....

3. ....

🪶 Write about a gift you recently received.

....

....

....

....

....

....

....

🎼 Musical Moment

What is your favorite song? Why is it your favorite?

🎼 Teaching Reflection

Describe a technology you mastered in order to improve your teaching or musicianship.

"*Music*,
like all of culture,
helps us to understand
our environment,
each other, and ourselves.
Culture
helps us to
imagine a better future.
Culture helps turn
"*them*" into "*us*."
And these things
have never been
more important."

— YO-YO MA

HABIT TRACKER

HABIT	1	2	3	4	5	6	7
_____	○	○	○	○	○	○	○
_____	○	○	○	○	○	○	○
_____	○	○	○	○	○	○	○
_____	○	○	○	○	○	○	○
_____	○	○	○	○	○	○	○
_____	○	○	○	○	○	○	○
_____	○	○	○	○	○	○	○
_____	○	○	○	○	○	○	○
_____	○	○	○	○	○	○	○
_____	○	○	○	○	○	○	○
_____	○	○	○	○	○	○	○
_____	○	○	○	○	○	○	○

NOTES

....
....
....
....
....
....

🍃 I felt appreciated when
_____

said/did

_____

_____

_____

_____

_____

_____

🍃 Draw or write about a dream you have for this year.

🍃 Write about a compliment you recently received.

. . . .
. . . .
. . . .
. . . .
. . . .
. . . .
. . . .

🎼 Musical Moment

Which composer are you especially grateful for? What makes them special?

....

....

....

....

....

....

....

🎼 Teaching Reflection

What type of culture do you want to create in your teaching space?

....

....

....

....

....

....

....

Song of Gratitude

Go to page 148 for Step One of your songwriting project.

> "It is the *supreme art* of the teacher to awaken joy in creative expression and knowledge."
>
> — ALBERT EINSTEIN

HABIT TRACKER

HABIT	1	2	3	4	5	6	7
_____	○	○	○	○	○	○	○
_____	○	○	○	○	○	○	○
_____	○	○	○	○	○	○	○
_____	○	○	○	○	○	○	○
_____	○	○	○	○	○	○	○
_____	○	○	○	○	○	○	○
_____	○	○	○	○	○	○	○
_____	○	○	○	○	○	○	○
_____	○	○	○	○	○	○	○
_____	○	○	○	○	○	○	○
_____	○	○	○	○	○	○	○
_____	○	○	○	○	○	○	○

NOTES

....
....
....
....
....
....

🪶 I experienced the joy of teaching music when

_____

_____

_____

_____

_____

_____

_____

_____

🪶 List three things you are curious about.

1. ....

2. ....

3. ....

🪶 How can you be kinder to yourself?

....

....

....

....

....

....

....

🎼 Musical Moment

Write about one experience in rehearsal or performance that sparked your soul.

....
....
....
....
....
....
....
....

🎼 Teaching Reflection

Write about a class/student that you look forward to teaching.

....
....
....
....
....
....
....

"With music, one's whole future life is *brightened.* This is such a treasure in life that it helps us over many troubles and difficulties. Music is nourishment, a comforting elixir. Music *multiplies* all that is *beautiful* and of value in life."

— ZOLTÁN KODÁLY

HABIT TRACKER

HABIT	1	2	3	4	5	6	7
_____	○	○	○	○	○	○	○
_____	○	○	○	○	○	○	○
_____	○	○	○	○	○	○	○
_____	○	○	○	○	○	○	○
_____	○	○	○	○	○	○	○
_____	○	○	○	○	○	○	○
_____	○	○	○	○	○	○	○
_____	○	○	○	○	○	○	○
_____	○	○	○	○	○	○	○
_____	○	○	○	○	○	○	○
_____	○	○	○	○	○	○	○
_____	○	○	○	○	○	○	○

NOTES

....
....
....
....
....
....

🍃 I am grateful that _____

made my job easier by

_____

_____

_____

_____

_____

_____

🍃 Sketch an image of a non-musical activity that you are grateful to enjoy.

🍃 Write about a new idea, project, or piece of music that you would like to pursue.

. . . .

. . . .

. . . .

. . . .

. . . .

. . . .

. . . .

🎼 Musical Moment

Write about three pieces of music you listened to in the past month and why you are glad you did.

🎼 Teaching Reflection

Write about a rehearsal or lesson plan that went better than expected.

"*Acknowledging the good* that is already in your life is the foundation for all abundance."

— ECKHART TOLLE

Excerpt(s) from *A NEW EARTH: AWAKENING TO YOUR LIFE'S PURPOSE* by Eckhart Tolle, Copyright © 2005 by Eckhart Tolle. Used by permission of Dutton, an imprint of Penguin Publishing Group, a division of Penguin Random House LLC. All rights reserved.

HABIT TRACKER

HABIT	1	2	3	4	5	6	7
_____	○	○	○	○	○	○	○
_____	○	○	○	○	○	○	○
_____	○	○	○	○	○	○	○
_____	○	○	○	○	○	○	○
_____	○	○	○	○	○	○	○
_____	○	○	○	○	○	○	○
_____	○	○	○	○	○	○	○
_____	○	○	○	○	○	○	○
_____	○	○	○	○	○	○	○
_____	○	○	○	○	○	○	○
_____	○	○	○	○	○	○	○
_____	○	○	○	○	○	○	○

NOTES

....
....
....
....
....
....

🪶 I am grateful to be a musician because

_____
_____
_____
_____
_____
_____
_____
_____

🪶 Write three good news "headlines" from this week.

1. ....

2. ....

3. ....

🪶 What is going well for you this week?

....
....
....
....
....
....
....

🎼 Musical Moment
Describe a live musical experience and how the experience affected you.

....
....
....
....
....
....
....
....

🎼 Teaching Reflection
What's your proudest teaching memory?

....
....
....
....
....
....
....
....

"You can't use up **creativity.** The more you use, the more you have."

— MAYA ANGELOU

Weekly
HABIT TRACKER

HABIT	1	2	3	4	5	6	7
_____	○	○	○	○	○	○	○
_____	○	○	○	○	○	○	○
_____	○	○	○	○	○	○	○
_____	○	○	○	○	○	○	○
_____	○	○	○	○	○	○	○
_____	○	○	○	○	○	○	○
_____	○	○	○	○	○	○	○
_____	○	○	○	○	○	○	○
_____	○	○	○	○	○	○	○
_____	○	○	○	○	○	○	○
_____	○	○	○	○	○	○	○
_____	○	○	○	○	○	○	○

NOTES

....
....
....
....
....
....

🪶 I feel most creative when I

_____

_____

_____

_____

_____

_____

_____

_____

🪶 Draw or write about a favorite resource in your "toolbox."

🪶 Who did you encourage today? How did it make you feel?

. . . .

. . . .

. . . .

. . . .

. . . .

. . . .

. . . .

Musical Moment
Write about a meaningful musical performance you participated in.

Teaching Reflection
Imagine you are the "ideal" teacher—what would you be doing more of? What would you be doing less of?

Song of Gratitude
Go to page 149 for Step Two of your songwriting project.

> "*Education* is the most *powerful* weapon which you can use to *change the world.*"
>
> — NELSON MANDELA

HABIT TRACKER

HABIT	1	2	3	4	5	6	7
_____	○	○	○	○	○	○	○
_____	○	○	○	○	○	○	○
_____	○	○	○	○	○	○	○
_____	○	○	○	○	○	○	○
_____	○	○	○	○	○	○	○
_____	○	○	○	○	○	○	○
_____	○	○	○	○	○	○	○
_____	○	○	○	○	○	○	○
_____	○	○	○	○	○	○	○
_____	○	○	○	○	○	○	○
_____	○	○	○	○	○	○	○
_____	○	○	○	○	○	○	○

NOTES

....
....
....
....
....
....

🍃 I could make my daily routine

_____

if I stopped/started

_____

_____

_____

_____

_____

_____

🍃 Be your own cheerleader!
What goals did you score this week?

1. ....

2. ....

3. ....

🍃 Write about a time when you stood up for what you thought was right, regardless of what other people believed.

. . . .

. . . .

. . . .

. . . .

. . . .

. . . .

. . . .

🎼 Musical Moment
What song lyrics or musical passages moved you recently?

....
....
....
....
....
....
....
....

🎼 Teaching Reflection
How do you see music education impacting students in other classes or parts of their lives?

....
....
....
....
....
....
....
....

"Teaching music is not my main purpose. I want to make *good citizens*. If children hear fine music from the day of their birth and learn to play it, they develop *sensitivity, discipline, and endurance*. They get a beautiful heart."

— SHINICHI SUZUKI

© 1983, 1985, 2012 Shinichi Suzuki
All Rights Administered by SUZUKI METHOD INTERNATIONAL / SUMMY-BIRCHARD, INC.
ALFRED MUSIC, Exclusive Print Distributor and Licensor for the World Excluding Japan.

HABIT TRACKER

HABIT	1	2	3	4	5	6	7
_____	○	○	○	○	○	○	○
_____	○	○	○	○	○	○	○
_____	○	○	○	○	○	○	○
_____	○	○	○	○	○	○	○
_____	○	○	○	○	○	○	○
_____	○	○	○	○	○	○	○
_____	○	○	○	○	○	○	○
_____	○	○	○	○	○	○	○
_____	○	○	○	○	○	○	○
_____	○	○	○	○	○	○	○
_____	○	○	○	○	○	○	○
_____	○	○	○	○	○	○	○

NOTES

....
....
....
....
....
....

🪶 I want to start

_____

because

_____

_____

_____

_____

_____

_____

🪶 Illustrate something you hope will be better by this time next year.

🪶 What non-musical activity are you most grateful for?

....
....
....
....
....
....
....

🎼 **Musical Moment**

When was the last time you explored new music or genres? What did you enjoy?

....
....
....
....
....
....
....
....

🎼 **Teaching Reflection**

Do you incorporate fun and playful activities into your teaching? Why or why not? Would your students agree with your answer?

....
....
....
....
....
....
....
....

"*Success* is to be measured not so much by the position that one has reached in life as by the obstacles which he has overcome while trying to succeed."

— BOOKER T. WASHINGTON

HABIT TRACKER

HABIT	1	2	3	4	5	6	7
_____	○	○	○	○	○	○	○
_____	○	○	○	○	○	○	○
_____	○	○	○	○	○	○	○
_____	○	○	○	○	○	○	○
_____	○	○	○	○	○	○	○
_____	○	○	○	○	○	○	○
_____	○	○	○	○	○	○	○
_____	○	○	○	○	○	○	○
_____	○	○	○	○	○	○	○
_____	○	○	○	○	○	○	○
_____	○	○	○	○	○	○	○
_____	○	○	○	○	○	○	○

NOTES

....
....
....
....
....
....

🍃 I gave without expectation to

_____

when I

_____

_____

_____

_____

_____

_____

🍃 List three resources that make teaching easier for you.

1. ....

2. ....

3. ....

🍃 What filled you up this week?

....

....

....

....

....

....

....

🎼 Musical Moment

Write about a time when music helped you through something difficult.

. . . .

. . . .

. . . .

. . . .

. . . .

. . . .

. . . .

. . . .

🎼 Teaching Reflection

What is the best teaching advice you have received?
How have you put this wisdom to use?

. . . .

. . . .

. . . .

. . . .

. . . .

. . . .

. . . .

. . . .

> "*Art, in itself, is an attempt to bring order out of chaos.*"
>
> — STEPHEN SONDHEIM

HABIT TRACKER

HABIT	1	2	3	4	5	6	7
_____	○	○	○	○	○	○	○
_____	○	○	○	○	○	○	○
_____	○	○	○	○	○	○	○
_____	○	○	○	○	○	○	○
_____	○	○	○	○	○	○	○
_____	○	○	○	○	○	○	○
_____	○	○	○	○	○	○	○
_____	○	○	○	○	○	○	○
_____	○	○	○	○	○	○	○
_____	○	○	○	○	○	○	○
_____	○	○	○	○	○	○	○
_____	○	○	○	○	○	○	○

NOTES

....
....
....
....
....
....

🪶 This week

_____

taught me

_____

_____

_____

_____

_____

_____

🪶 Design a personal affirmation or mantra.

🪶 How do you practice self care?

. . . .

. . . .

. . . .

. . . .

. . . .

. . . .

. . . .

Musical Moment

Write about three pieces of music you listened to in the past month and why you are glad you did.

....

....

....

....

....

....

Teaching Reflection

How would your school and students be impacted if the music program was eliminated?

....

....

....

....

....

....

Song of Gratitude

Go to page 149 for Step Three of your songwriting project.

"He who is not *courageous* enough to *take risks* will accomplish nothing in life."

— MUHAMMAD ALI

HABIT TRACKER

HABIT	1	2	3	4	5	6	7
_____	○	○	○	○	○	○	○
_____	○	○	○	○	○	○	○
_____	○	○	○	○	○	○	○
_____	○	○	○	○	○	○	○
_____	○	○	○	○	○	○	○
_____	○	○	○	○	○	○	○
_____	○	○	○	○	○	○	○
_____	○	○	○	○	○	○	○
_____	○	○	○	○	○	○	○
_____	○	○	○	○	○	○	○
_____	○	○	○	○	○	○	○
_____	○	○	○	○	○	○	○

NOTES

....
....
....
....
....
....

🪶 The last thing I was a beginner at was

_____

_____

and I felt

_____

_____

_____

_____

_____

🪶 What three song titles would make up the soundtrack of your week?

1. ....

2. ....

3. ....

🪶 What did you learn about this week that will improve your life?

....

....

....

....

....

....

....

🎼 Musical Moment

How did you form your taste in music? Who influenced your listening choices?

....
....
....
....
....
....
....
....

🎼 Teaching Reflection

What milestones do you look forward to reaching with a student or an ensemble?

....
....
....
....
....
....
....
....

"*The easiest way* to avoid wrong notes is to never open your mouth and *sing.* What a mistake that would be."

— PETE SEEGER

Weekly
HABIT TRACKER

HABIT	1	2	3	4	5	6	7
_____	○	○	○	○	○	○	○
_____	○	○	○	○	○	○	○
_____	○	○	○	○	○	○	○
_____	○	○	○	○	○	○	○
_____	○	○	○	○	○	○	○
_____	○	○	○	○	○	○	○
_____	○	○	○	○	○	○	○
_____	○	○	○	○	○	○	○
_____	○	○	○	○	○	○	○
_____	○	○	○	○	○	○	○
_____	○	○	○	○	○	○	○
_____	○	○	○	○	○	○	○

NOTES

....
....
....
....
....
....

🍃 One quality I admire in
_____

is

_____

_____

_____

_____

_____

_____

_____

🍃 Draw something you are optimistic about in the near future.

🍃 Who do you look to for encouragement? Why?

. . . .

. . . .

. . . .

. . . .

. . . .

. . . .

. . . .

Musical Moment

What opportunities have opened up to you by being a musician?

....
....
....
....
....
....
....
....

Teaching Reflection

Write about a teaching failure that you are grateful for, and what you learned from it.

....
....
....
....
....
....
....
....

"I am not a *teacher,* but an *awakener.*"

— ROBERT FROST

HABIT TRACKER

HABIT	1	2	3	4	5	6	7
_____	○	○	○	○	○	○	○
_____	○	○	○	○	○	○	○
_____	○	○	○	○	○	○	○
_____	○	○	○	○	○	○	○
_____	○	○	○	○	○	○	○
_____	○	○	○	○	○	○	○
_____	○	○	○	○	○	○	○
_____	○	○	○	○	○	○	○
_____	○	○	○	○	○	○	○
_____	○	○	○	○	○	○	○
_____	○	○	○	○	○	○	○
_____	○	○	○	○	○	○	○

NOTES

....
....
....
....
....
....

🪶 I am grateful for

_____

because he/she/they

_____

_____

_____

_____

_____

_____

🪶 List three things you can't buy that you are grateful for.

1. ....

2. ....

3. ....

🪶 What did you accomplish this week? How did you celebrate?

....

....

....

....

....

....

....

🎼 Musical Moment

Imagine you can only listen to three pieces of music for the rest of your life. Which pieces will you choose, and why?

....

....

....

....

....

....

....

....

🎼 Teaching Reflection

Name the biggest obstacle you are facing with one of your classes. List three things you can do to change it.

....

....

....

....

....

....

....

....

"In everyone's life, at some time, our *inner fire* goes out. It is then burst *into flame* by an encounter with another human being. We should all be thankful for those who *rekindle* the *inner spirit.*"

— ALBERT SCHWEITZER

HABIT TRACKER

HABIT	1	2	3	4	5	6	7
_____	○	○	○	○	○	○	○
_____	○	○	○	○	○	○	○
_____	○	○	○	○	○	○	○
_____	○	○	○	○	○	○	○
_____	○	○	○	○	○	○	○
_____	○	○	○	○	○	○	○
_____	○	○	○	○	○	○	○
_____	○	○	○	○	○	○	○
_____	○	○	○	○	○	○	○
_____	○	○	○	○	○	○	○
_____	○	○	○	○	○	○	○
_____	○	○	○	○	○	○	○

NOTES

....
....
....
....
....
....

🌿 I encouraged

_____

when I

_____

_____

_____

_____

_____

_____

_____

🌿 Design the book cover for your life story.

🌿 Who or what in your life are you happy to have made space for? What was the impact?

....
....
....
....
....
....
....

♪ Musical Moment
What skills have you developed as a musican that help you in other parts of life?

♪ Teaching Reflection
Are you intentional about allowing opportunities for students to improvise? How does your comfort level with improvising shape their experience?

Song of Gratitude
Go to page 150 for Step Four of your songwriting project.

"When eating fruit, *remember* the one *who planted* the tree."

— VIETNAMESE PROVERB

HABIT TRACKER

HABIT	1	2	3	4	5	6	7
_____	○	○	○	○	○	○	○
_____	○	○	○	○	○	○	○
_____	○	○	○	○	○	○	○
_____	○	○	○	○	○	○	○
_____	○	○	○	○	○	○	○
_____	○	○	○	○	○	○	○
_____	○	○	○	○	○	○	○
_____	○	○	○	○	○	○	○
_____	○	○	○	○	○	○	○
_____	○	○	○	○	○	○	○
_____	○	○	○	○	○	○	○
_____	○	○	○	○	○	○	○

NOTES

....
....
....
....
....
....

🪶 No matter what happens,
I believe

_____

_____

_____

_____

_____

_____

_____

🪶 What are the three best decisions you've made in your life?

1. ....

2. ....

3. ....

🪶 What are you scared to do? How can you overcome your fear?

....

....

....

....

....

....

....

🎼 Musical Moment
Write about your musical mentors and how they impacted your teaching.

....

....

....

....

....

....

....

....

🎼 Teaching Reflection
What are you most excited about in your next concert/performance?

....

....

....

....

....

....

....

....

"Music *washes* away from *the soul* the dust of everyday life."

— BERTHOLD AUERBACH

HABIT TRACKER

HABIT	1	2	3	4	5	6	7
_____	○	○	○	○	○	○	○
_____	○	○	○	○	○	○	○
_____	○	○	○	○	○	○	○
_____	○	○	○	○	○	○	○
_____	○	○	○	○	○	○	○
_____	○	○	○	○	○	○	○
_____	○	○	○	○	○	○	○
_____	○	○	○	○	○	○	○
_____	○	○	○	○	○	○	○
_____	○	○	○	○	○	○	○
_____	○	○	○	○	○	○	○
_____	○	○	○	○	○	○	○

NOTES

....
....
....
....
....
....

🍃 I am always grateful for
_____

because
_____
_____
_____
_____
_____
_____
_____

🍃 Illustrate something that makes you lose track of time.

🍃 How are you making a difference in this world?

....
....
....
....
....
....
....

🎼 Musical Moment

Write about three pieces of music you listened to in the past month and why you are glad you did.

....
....
....
....
....
....
....
....
....
....

🎼 Teaching Reflection

Choose an experience from this week to save as a snapshot in your teaching scrapbook. What made this moment memorable or special?

....
....
....
....
....
....
....

"There is *music* in every child. The teacher's job is to *find it* and *nurture it.*"

— FRANCES CLARK

HABIT TRACKER

HABIT	1	2	3	4	5	6	7
_____	○	○	○	○	○	○	○
_____	○	○	○	○	○	○	○
_____	○	○	○	○	○	○	○
_____	○	○	○	○	○	○	○
_____	○	○	○	○	○	○	○
_____	○	○	○	○	○	○	○
_____	○	○	○	○	○	○	○
_____	○	○	○	○	○	○	○
_____	○	○	○	○	○	○	○
_____	○	○	○	○	○	○	○
_____	○	○	○	○	○	○	○
_____	○	○	○	○	○	○	○

NOTES

....
....
....
....
....
....

🌿 This week I moved toward my goal of

_____

by

_____

_____

_____

_____

_____

_____

🌿 List three things you want to try but haven't yet.

1. ....

2. ....

3. ....

🌿 What were you scared to do but are grateful to have done?

....

....

....

....

....

....

....

🎼 **Musical Moment**

Write a review of a new album you have listened to.

....
....
....
....
....
....
....
....

🎼 **Teaching Reflection**

Describe a positive choice you have made that brings you closer to being the teacher you want to be.

....
....
....
....
....
....
....
....

"*Music* is a more potent instrument than any other for education, because *rhythm* and *harmony* find their way into the inward places of *the soul.*"

— PLATO

HABIT TRACKER

HABIT	1	2	3	4	5	6	7
_____	○	○	○	○	○	○	○
_____	○	○	○	○	○	○	○
_____	○	○	○	○	○	○	○
_____	○	○	○	○	○	○	○
_____	○	○	○	○	○	○	○
_____	○	○	○	○	○	○	○
_____	○	○	○	○	○	○	○
_____	○	○	○	○	○	○	○
_____	○	○	○	○	○	○	○
_____	○	○	○	○	○	○	○
_____	○	○	○	○	○	○	○
_____	○	○	○	○	○	○	○

NOTES

....
....
....
....
....
....

🍃 _____

helped me this week when

_____

_____

_____

_____

_____

_____

_____

🍃 Draw or write the things that fill you up.

🍃 What parts of your life feel "in harmony?"

....

....

....

....

....

....

....

🎼 Musical Moment
Write about the musical accomplishment you are most proud of.

....

....

....

....

....

....

....

🎼 Teaching Reflection
Describe something you had to learn the hard way about teaching.

....

....

....

....

....

....

Song of Gratitude
Go to page 151 for Step Five of your songwriting project.

"It is the *artists* of the world, the feelers and thinkers, who will ultimately *save us,* who can articulate, educate, defy, insist, sing, and shout the *big dreams.* Only the artists can turn the not-yet into *reality.*"

— LEONARD BERNSTEIN

HABIT TRACKER

HABIT	1	2	3	4	5	6	7
_____	○	○	○	○	○	○	○
_____	○	○	○	○	○	○	○
_____	○	○	○	○	○	○	○
_____	○	○	○	○	○	○	○
_____	○	○	○	○	○	○	○
_____	○	○	○	○	○	○	○
_____	○	○	○	○	○	○	○
_____	○	○	○	○	○	○	○
_____	○	○	○	○	○	○	○
_____	○	○	○	○	○	○	○
_____	○	○	○	○	○	○	○
_____	○	○	○	○	○	○	○

NOTES

....
....
....
....
....
....

🌿 I'm grateful I was able to spend time with

_____

_____

_____

_____

_____

_____

_____

_____

_____

🌿 Give yourself three compliments.

1. ....

2. ....

3. ....

🌿 What boundaries have you set that help you maintain balance in your life?

....

....

....

....

....

....

....

Musical Moment

What is the purpose of music in your life?

Teaching Reflection

How has your ensemble (or an individual student) improved from this point last year?

"A teacher affects *eternity*; he can never tell where his *influence* stops."

— HENRY B. ADAMS

HABIT TRACKER

HABIT	1	2	3	4	5	6	7
_____	○	○	○	○	○	○	○
_____	○	○	○	○	○	○	○
_____	○	○	○	○	○	○	○
_____	○	○	○	○	○	○	○
_____	○	○	○	○	○	○	○
_____	○	○	○	○	○	○	○
_____	○	○	○	○	○	○	○
_____	○	○	○	○	○	○	○
_____	○	○	○	○	○	○	○
_____	○	○	○	○	○	○	○
_____	○	○	○	○	○	○	○
_____	○	○	○	○	○	○	○

NOTES

....
....
....
....
....
....

🌿 I felt good about my teaching when

_____

said/did

_____

_____

_____

_____

_____

_____

🌿 Draw a symbol or item that represents gratitude.

🌿 Write about an event that left you feeling inspired or energized.

. . . .

. . . .

. . . .

. . . .

. . . .

. . . .

. . . .

🎼 Musical Moment
Who are some musicians you admire? Why do they inspire you?

....
....
....
....
....
....
....
....

🎼 Teaching Reflection
How can you do more to honor the culture and history of your students?

....
....
....
....
....
....
....
....

"Feeling gratitude and not *expressing it* is like wrapping a present and not *giving it.*"

— WILLIAM ARTHUR WARD

HABIT TRACKER

HABIT	1	2	3	4	5	6	7
_____	○	○	○	○	○	○	○
_____	○	○	○	○	○	○	○
_____	○	○	○	○	○	○	○
_____	○	○	○	○	○	○	○
_____	○	○	○	○	○	○	○
_____	○	○	○	○	○	○	○
_____	○	○	○	○	○	○	○
_____	○	○	○	○	○	○	○
_____	○	○	○	○	○	○	○
_____	○	○	○	○	○	○	○
_____	○	○	○	○	○	○	○
_____	○	○	○	○	○	○	○

NOTES

....
....
....
....
....
....

🌿 I am happy about

_____

because

_____

_____

_____

_____

_____

_____

🌿 Name three people you can always count on to laugh with.

1. ....

2. ....

3. ....

🌿 Who are you taking for granted? What can you do to show more appreciation for this person?

....

....

....

....

....

....

....

🎼 Musical Moment

Choose a book to make into a musical. What style(s) of music would you use? List some song titles.

🎼 Teaching Reflection

Write a thank you note to someone who has impacted your teaching. This could be an author, a musician, or someone you know.

"A problem is *your chance* to do *your best.*"

— DUKE ELLINGTON

Weekly
HABIT TRACKER

HABIT	1	2	3	4	5	6	7
_____	○	○	○	○	○	○	○
_____	○	○	○	○	○	○	○
_____	○	○	○	○	○	○	○
_____	○	○	○	○	○	○	○
_____	○	○	○	○	○	○	○
_____	○	○	○	○	○	○	○
_____	○	○	○	○	○	○	○
_____	○	○	○	○	○	○	○
_____	○	○	○	○	○	○	○
_____	○	○	○	○	○	○	○
_____	○	○	○	○	○	○	○
_____	○	○	○	○	○	○	○

NOTES

....
....
....
....
....
....

🪶 I feel grateful for my career because

_____
_____
_____
_____
_____
_____
_____
_____
_____

🪶 Draw or write the gifts you received this week.

🪶 Write about a time when things were difficult but you didn't give up.

. . . .
. . . .
. . . .
. . . .
. . . .
. . . .
. . . .

🎼 Musical Moment
Write about three pieces of music you listened to in the past month and why you are glad you did.

....

....

....

....

....

....

....

🎼 Teaching Reflection
Describe an unexpected student reaction that made you smile this week.

....

....

....

....

....

....

Song of Gratitude
Go to page 151 for Step Six of your songwriting project.

"It is my firm conviction that mankind will *live the happier* when it has learned to *live with music* more worthily. Whoever works to promote this end, in one way or another, has *not lived in vain.*"

— ZOLTÁN KODÁLY

HABIT TRACKER

HABIT	1	2	3	4	5	6	7
_____	○	○	○	○	○	○	○
_____	○	○	○	○	○	○	○
_____	○	○	○	○	○	○	○
_____	○	○	○	○	○	○	○
_____	○	○	○	○	○	○	○
_____	○	○	○	○	○	○	○
_____	○	○	○	○	○	○	○
_____	○	○	○	○	○	○	○
_____	○	○	○	○	○	○	○
_____	○	○	○	○	○	○	○
_____	○	○	○	○	○	○	○
_____	○	○	○	○	○	○	○

NOTES

....
....
....
....
....
....

🪶 This week I am better at

_____

than I was last week.

_____

_____

_____

_____

_____

_____

🪶 List three ways you will make tomorrow even better.

1. ....

2. ....

3. ....

🪶 How could saying "no" to something allow you to give more of yourself?

....

....

....

....

....

....

....

Musical Moment

Recall a time in your musical training when a concept or skill finally "clicked" for you.

Teaching Reflection

Write about something you learned this week that will improve your teaching.

"As we *express* our gratitude, we must never forget that the *highest appreciation* is not to utter words, but to *live* by them."

— JOHN F. KENNEDY

HABIT TRACKER

HABIT	1	2	3	4	5	6	7
_____	○	○	○	○	○	○	○
_____	○	○	○	○	○	○	○
_____	○	○	○	○	○	○	○
_____	○	○	○	○	○	○	○
_____	○	○	○	○	○	○	○
_____	○	○	○	○	○	○	○
_____	○	○	○	○	○	○	○
_____	○	○	○	○	○	○	○
_____	○	○	○	○	○	○	○
_____	○	○	○	○	○	○	○
_____	○	○	○	○	○	○	○
_____	○	○	○	○	○	○	○

NOTES

....
....
....
....
....
....

🪶 I experienced kindness today when

_____

_____

_____

_____

_____

_____

_____

_____

🪶 Draw something you can't live without.

🪶 What role in your life makes you feel like your most authentic self? How can that feeling expand to other parts of life?

....

....

....

....

....

....

🎼 Musical Moment
What is the most rewarding aspect of being a musician?

🎼 Teaching Reflection
What progress have you made with a group or an individual student that you are proud of?

"Music education *opens doors* that help children pass from school *into the world* around them — a world of work, culture, intellectual activity, and human involvement. *The future* of our nation depends on providing our children with a complete education that *includes music.*"

— GERALD FORD

HABIT TRACKER

HABIT	1	2	3	4	5	6	7
_____	○	○	○	○	○	○	○
_____	○	○	○	○	○	○	○
_____	○	○	○	○	○	○	○
_____	○	○	○	○	○	○	○
_____	○	○	○	○	○	○	○
_____	○	○	○	○	○	○	○
_____	○	○	○	○	○	○	○
_____	○	○	○	○	○	○	○
_____	○	○	○	○	○	○	○
_____	○	○	○	○	○	○	○
_____	○	○	○	○	○	○	○
_____	○	○	○	○	○	○	○

NOTES

....
....
....
....
....
....

🪶 The silver lining about

_____

is that

_____

_____

_____

_____

_____

_____

_____

🪶 List three people you are grateful to know.

1. ....

2. ....

3. ....

🪶 What happened this week that required courage?

....

....

....

....

....

....

....

🎼 **Musical Moment**

What makes a piece of music worthwhile to you?

🎼 **Teaching Reflection**

What tradition are you most proud of in your program/school?

"In recognizing the *humanity* of our fellow beings, we pay ourselves the highest tribute."

— THURGOOD MARSHALL

HABIT TRACKER

HABIT	1	2	3	4	5	6	7
_____	○	○	○	○	○	○	○
_____	○	○	○	○	○	○	○
_____	○	○	○	○	○	○	○
_____	○	○	○	○	○	○	○
_____	○	○	○	○	○	○	○
_____	○	○	○	○	○	○	○
_____	○	○	○	○	○	○	○
_____	○	○	○	○	○	○	○
_____	○	○	○	○	○	○	○
_____	○	○	○	○	○	○	○
_____	○	○	○	○	○	○	○
_____	○	○	○	○	○	○	○

NOTES

....
....
....
....
....
....

🍃 I experienced the joy of teaching when

_____

_____

_____

_____

_____

_____

_____

🍃 Color this mandala.

🍃 What challenges did you face this week, and how did you overcome them?

. . . .

. . . .

. . . .

. . . .

. . . .

. . . .

🎼 Musical Moment
Explain where your love of music comes from.

. . . .

. . . .

. . . .

. . . .

. . . .

. . . .

. . . .

🎼 Teaching Reflection
If your classroom/studio was "perfect," how would it look the same or different as it does now?

. . . .

. . . .

. . . .

. . . .

. . . .

. . . .

Song of Gratitude
Go to page 151 for Step Seven of your songwriting project.

"*A life* is not important except in *the impact* it has on other lives."

— JACKIE ROBINSON

HABIT TRACKER

HABIT	1	2	3	4	5	6	7
_____	○	○	○	○	○	○	○
_____	○	○	○	○	○	○	○
_____	○	○	○	○	○	○	○
_____	○	○	○	○	○	○	○
_____	○	○	○	○	○	○	○
_____	○	○	○	○	○	○	○
_____	○	○	○	○	○	○	○
_____	○	○	○	○	○	○	○
_____	○	○	○	○	○	○	○
_____	○	○	○	○	○	○	○
_____	○	○	○	○	○	○	○
_____	○	○	○	○	○	○	○

NOTES

....
....
....
....
....
....

🌿 When I express my gratitude to others, I feel more

_____

_____

_____

_____

_____

_____

_____

🌿 List three of your music education mentors.

1. ....

2. ....

3. ....

🌿 How do you show gratitude to others?

....

....

....

....

....

....

....

Musical Moment

How do you stay connected to your personal love of music?

Teaching Reflection

Write about a student that you made a difference for this week.

"You're not obligated to win. You're obligated to **keep trying** to do the **best you can** every day."

— MARIAN WRIGHT EDELMAN

HABIT TRACKER

HABIT	1	2	3	4	5	6	7
_____	○	○	○	○	○	○	○
_____	○	○	○	○	○	○	○
_____	○	○	○	○	○	○	○
_____	○	○	○	○	○	○	○
_____	○	○	○	○	○	○	○
_____	○	○	○	○	○	○	○
_____	○	○	○	○	○	○	○
_____	○	○	○	○	○	○	○
_____	○	○	○	○	○	○	○
_____	○	○	○	○	○	○	○
_____	○	○	○	○	○	○	○
_____	○	○	○	○	○	○	○

NOTES

....
....
....
....
....
....

🪶 I am grateful for

_____

because

_____

_____

_____

_____

_____

_____

_____

🪶 Draw a scene of your "happy place."

🪶 How do you feed off the creative energy of those around you?

....

....

....

....

....

....

....

🎼 Musical Moment

Write about three pieces of music you listened to in the past month and why you are glad you did.

....

....

....

....

....

....

....

....

🎼 Teaching Reflection

What are you teaching your students that will help them no matter what career path they choose?

....

....

....

....

....

....

....

....

"It's not *joy* that makes us grateful, it's *gratitude* that makes us joyful."

— DAVID STEINDL-RAST

HABIT TRACKER

HABIT	1	2	3	4	5	6	7
_____	○	○	○	○	○	○	○
_____	○	○	○	○	○	○	○
_____	○	○	○	○	○	○	○
_____	○	○	○	○	○	○	○
_____	○	○	○	○	○	○	○
_____	○	○	○	○	○	○	○
_____	○	○	○	○	○	○	○
_____	○	○	○	○	○	○	○
_____	○	○	○	○	○	○	○
_____	○	○	○	○	○	○	○
_____	○	○	○	○	○	○	○
_____	○	○	○	○	○	○	○

NOTES

....
....
....
....
....
....

🪶 I am grateful for my love of

_____

because

_____

_____

_____

_____

_____

_____

🪶 List three ways you show your appreciation to others.

1. ....

2. ....

3. ....

🪶 What are you taking for granted?

....

....

....

....

....

....

....

🎼 Musical Moment

Name a song that always brings to mind a specific memory. What is the memory, and how is the song connected?

....

....

....

....

....

....

....

....

....

🎼 Teaching Reflection

How have you or your program been supported by your administration or parents?

....

....

....

....

....

....

....

....

....

"If you are building a house and a nail breaks, do you stop building or do you change the nail?"

— RWANDAN PROVERB

Weekly
HABIT TRACKER

HABIT	1	2	3	4	5	6	7
_____	○	○	○	○	○	○	○
_____	○	○	○	○	○	○	○
_____	○	○	○	○	○	○	○
_____	○	○	○	○	○	○	○
_____	○	○	○	○	○	○	○
_____	○	○	○	○	○	○	○
_____	○	○	○	○	○	○	○
_____	○	○	○	○	○	○	○
_____	○	○	○	○	○	○	○
_____	○	○	○	○	○	○	○
_____	○	○	○	○	○	○	○
_____	○	○	○	○	○	○	○

NOTES

....
....
....
....
....
....

🍃 I will show my appreciation to

_____

by

_____

_____

_____

_____

_____

_____

🍃 Fill this space with positive images or words.

🍃 Describe what you are proud to have done this week.

....

....

....

....

....

....

....

Musical Moment

What changes have you made in your musical journey that have had a positive impact on your musicianship?

....

....

....

....

....

....

....

....

Teaching Reflection

What was your best teaching moment this week, and how can you have more moments like it?

....

....

....

....

....

....

....

Song of Gratitude
Go to page 152 for Step Eight of your songwriting project.

"There are only two ways to *live* your life. One is as though nothing is a miracle. The other is as though *everything is a miracle.*"

— ALBERT EINSTEIN

HABIT TRACKER

HABIT	1	2	3	4	5	6	7
_____	○	○	○	○	○	○	○
_____	○	○	○	○	○	○	○
_____	○	○	○	○	○	○	○
_____	○	○	○	○	○	○	○
_____	○	○	○	○	○	○	○
_____	○	○	○	○	○	○	○
_____	○	○	○	○	○	○	○
_____	○	○	○	○	○	○	○
_____	○	○	○	○	○	○	○
_____	○	○	○	○	○	○	○
_____	○	○	○	○	○	○	○
_____	○	○	○	○	○	○	○

NOTES

....
....
....
....
....
....

🪶 My reason to smile today is

_____

_____

_____

_____

_____

_____

_____

🪶 List three ways you have grown as a person.

1. ....

2. ....

3. ....

🪶 Describe what you are proud to have not done this week.

....

....

....

....

....

....

....

Musical Moment
What's the first song you learned? Who taught it to you? What do you remember about learning it?

Teaching Reflection
Write about another teacher who is a lifeline for you.

"The *language* of music is common to all generations and nations; it is *understood* by everybody, since it is understood *with the heart.*"

— GIOACHINO ROSSINI

HABIT TRACKER

HABIT	1	2	3	4	5	6	7
_____	○	○	○	○	○	○	○
_____	○	○	○	○	○	○	○
_____	○	○	○	○	○	○	○
_____	○	○	○	○	○	○	○
_____	○	○	○	○	○	○	○
_____	○	○	○	○	○	○	○
_____	○	○	○	○	○	○	○
_____	○	○	○	○	○	○	○
_____	○	○	○	○	○	○	○
_____	○	○	○	○	○	○	○
_____	○	○	○	○	○	○	○
_____	○	○	○	○	○	○	○

NOTES

....
....
....
....
....
....

🌿 I am grateful for access to
_____

because
_____
_____
_____
_____
_____
_____
_____

🌿 Draw a picture of something in nature that you appreciate.

🌿 What mistake or failure are you most grateful for?

....
....
....
....
....
....
....

🎼 Musical Moment

If you could learn to play one more instrument, what would it be and why?

....

....

....

....

....

....

....

....

🎼 Teaching Reflection

What do you want your students to remember about you?

....

....

....

....

....

....

....

....

"Without music, *life* would be a mistake."

— FRIEDRICH NIETZSCHE

HABIT TRACKER

HABIT	1	2	3	4	5	6	7
_____	○	○	○	○	○	○	○
_____	○	○	○	○	○	○	○
_____	○	○	○	○	○	○	○
_____	○	○	○	○	○	○	○
_____	○	○	○	○	○	○	○
_____	○	○	○	○	○	○	○
_____	○	○	○	○	○	○	○
_____	○	○	○	○	○	○	○
_____	○	○	○	○	○	○	○
_____	○	○	○	○	○	○	○
_____	○	○	○	○	○	○	○
_____	○	○	○	○	○	○	○

NOTES

....
....
....
....
....
....

🪶 This week, I'm grateful I had the opportunity to

_____

_____

_____

_____

_____

_____

_____

🪶 List three reasons to be excited about the future.

1. ....

2. ....

3. ....

🪶 Write about something you have worked hard to achieve.

. . . .

. . . .

. . . .

. . . .

. . . .

. . . .

. . . .

Musical Moment
What personal musical achievement are you most proud of from this year?

Teaching Reflection
Describe a time when you witnessed a "light bulb" moment for one of your students.

"The art of
being happy
lies in the power
of extracting
happiness
from
common things."

— HENRY WARD BEECHER

HABIT TRACKER

HABIT	1	2	3	4	5	6	7
_____	○	○	○	○	○	○	○
_____	○	○	○	○	○	○	○
_____	○	○	○	○	○	○	○
_____	○	○	○	○	○	○	○
_____	○	○	○	○	○	○	○
_____	○	○	○	○	○	○	○
_____	○	○	○	○	○	○	○
_____	○	○	○	○	○	○	○
_____	○	○	○	○	○	○	○
_____	○	○	○	○	○	○	○
_____	○	○	○	○	○	○	○
_____	○	○	○	○	○	○	○

NOTES

....
....
....
....
....
....

🌿 Music makes my life more
_____

because it
_____
_____
_____
_____
_____
_____
_____

🌿 Draw or write the "baggage" you are ready to let go of.

🌿 Write about what you have learned by practicing gratitude with this journal.

....
....
....
....
....
....
....

🎼 Musical Moment
How have you grown as a musician this year?

....

....

....

....

....

....

....

🎼 Teaching Reflection
Imagine you are asked to choose three items from your classroom to include in a time capsule. What do you choose, and why?

....

....

....

....

....

....

Song of Gratitude
Go to page 152 to complete your songwriting project.

Song of Gratitude

This composition project is constructed to help you find the music inside and all around you. Use it as a tool to explore your own creativity and expression. The process is broken down into nine steps (roughly one for each teaching month) so that you have plenty of time to consider and develop each aspect along the way.

This exercise may take you slightly out of your comfort zone. That's great! If you've never explored composing, you may learn some things about yourself. Embrace the process as a way to open a new creative space.

There is no one "right" way to compose, but this project provides a commonly used, logical sequence. Use the instructions as the framework or just a starting point for your own writing, and then feel free to adapt the steps into a composition project for your students.

STEP 1 Establish Your Vocabulary

Find a time and place that is free from distractions. Focus your attention on words (or word combinations) surrounding the theme of gratitude. Do not make judgements about any terms or phrases that come up. Just write them down—you can edit later. As a starting point, reflect on what you have recorded in this gratitude journal. Include single words, sayings, and quotes that feel personal to you. Create a vocabulary list below.

Tools: A thesaurus may offer some inspiring synonyms for your vocabulary list.

STEP 2 Develop a Poem

Read the words and phrases you curated in step 1, and begin to assemble a gratitude poem. Consider writing separate ideas on individual index cards, and lay them out in different ways. Rearrange the vocabulary to garner the most meaning and create a smooth rhythmic flow. Narrow your ideas down to a brief four-line poem. Write your completed poem below.

Tools: A rhyming dictionary will present even more possibilities.

LINE 1: _____

LINE 2: _____

LINE 3: _____

LINE 4: _____

STEP 3 Find the Rhythm

Read your gratitude poem aloud several times. If you listen closely, you may discover a built-in meter. Choose a time signature and write that in the box at the left. Next, examine the rhythm, structure, and cadence of each line. Use the single-line staff below to notate your spoken rhythm (think Sprechstimme or rap). Set your words in a natural way to ensure good prosody. Place stressed syllables on strong beats, and less important words (like articles) on weak beats, as shorter durations, or anacrusically. After you've noted the rhythm and added bar lines, write the syllables of your text underneath.

Tools: Use a dictionary to correctly hyphenate multi-syllable words.

 CONTINUED

STEP 4 Write a Melody

Your melody can be designed for any instrument. If not composing for voice, consider your vocabulary and rhythmic poem to be inspiration. Perform the poem out loud with emotion. Notice where your voice naturally rises and falls; a tune might already be implied. Think about how the shape of a melody can garner meaning. Most memorable tunes are built with question/answer (or antecedent/consequent) phrases. The answer usually ends on the tonic, and the question on another scale degree, such as the dominant. The two phrases should relate to one another. Allow yourself creative space to improvise freely, crafting a tune to match your rhythm and intent. Notice what key you naturally are drawn to—that's probably the one. Provide the instrument name, clef, key, and time signature, and then notate your melody.

Tools: Notate your melody using composition software such as Finale or the Compose app in SmartMusic (free at smartmusic.com).

INSTRUMENT: _____

STEP 5 Harmonize Your Tune

Believe it or not, your melody naturally implies underlying harmonics. So, let's reveal them! Begin with simple chords played on a keyboard or fretted instrument. As a music teacher, you know that the tonic chord is probably the place to both start and end. From there, try common chord progressions, and experiment with how various harmonies fit your melody. In a simple composition, most melodic notes will be chord tones (those within basic triads), with just a few passing tones or embellishments. For something more complex, try adding a 7th or 9th. The sonorities you design will shape the mood of the composition—tonal harmonies may be best to create a feeling of gratitude. When you are happy with the progression, add chord names above each measure of your melody in step 4.

Tools: Consult a chord progression guide such as Basic Chord Progressions *by Dick Weissman (Alfred #2220) to become familiar with commonly used harmonic sequences.*

STEP 6 Establish Your Vocabulary

Just as your vocabulary list provided a framework for the poem, your chord progression from step 5 will be the basis for the next part of this process. It's time to develop a supportive accompaniment based on the chords you selected. Of course, accompaniments can take many different forms. You may use a single instrument to form a duet, or several to add more color and timbre. A keyboard part might feature a bass line in the left hand and arpeggios in the right. A guitar, ukulele, or autoharp could perform rhythmic strum patterns. If you are drawn to the idea of a realized homophonic harmonization, consider choral voices, woodwinds, strings, or brasses. There is no wrong choice. Take your time and experiment until you are pleased.

Tools: Add additional instruments below the notated melody in your digital score using composition software such as Finale or the Compose app in SmartMusic (free at smartmusic.com).

STEP 7 Find a Form

This step is extremely flexible, and might even be optional. How is your piece coming along? Do you have a "main section" that has come together? Perhaps you'd enjoy expanding your composition! Here are some ideas. Write a brief introduction with logical sonorities that lead the ear to your tune. That same 2–4 bar motive might also provide a final outro, or even an interlude that transitions to a new section. If you desire a contrasting refrain, verse, or bridge, follow the first six steps of this project again. A few simple suggestions: B sections often begin on the subdominant chord or shift to the relative minor.

Tools: Continue to notate your developing piece using composition software such as Finale or the Compose app in SmartMusic (free at smartmusic.com).

 CONTINUED

STEP 8 Evaluate, Edit, and Arrange

For this step, consider yourself a music editor, and an arranger as well. If you have been using notation software, it will be easy to listen and evaluate your progress. Listen, listen again, step away, then listen some more. This is self-reflection at its best. Identify things you like about your song, and perhaps a couple of places that you'd like to improve. In addition to correcting little details, be sure to evaluate the entire song's effect. Remember, the greatest compositions provide a journey. Add dynamics, articulations, nuances in tempo, varied textures, etc., to create a composition with a clear starting place, a bit of growth, an emotional highpoint, and some kind of conclusion. Whether you end your journey as "settled" or "searching," consider the final measures as a summary, which can be achieved by repeating the final (or most important) thought again, perhaps with rhythmic augmentation or in a more reflective manner. This piece is about you, so your choices need not follow any traditional constructs. The only "rule" here is that the composition should be a sincere reflection of your gratitude.

Tools: Create and save different edits/versions of your piece using composition software such as Finale or the Compose app in SmartMusic (free at smartmusic.com).

STEP 9 Share Your Song

Sharing your song is the important final step in this process. It may require courage on your part, and for some, it will be an exercise in letting go of perfectionism. Allow yourself to be vulnerable as a way to spur your personal growth. Ask others to listen to the song and give you feedback, or share it with students to perform in class. The act of sharing your composition may spark others to tap into their own creativity.

Tools: Upload a MusicXML file of your work to SmartMusic and take advantage of the music sharing feature.

Reflect

Take a moment to acknowledge your achievement—you've done something amazing!

- What have you learned through this composition process?
- What was the biggest challenge along the way?
- Which of the nine steps brought you the greatest sense of accomplishment? Pride? Joy?

> *If you discovered that you enjoy writing music, keep going and growing! And someday when you have composed a fully developed work, we invite you to submit it for review at Alfred Music by visiting alfred.com/submissions. We welcome submissions from music teachers, and never discriminate on the basis of race, color, national origin, age, or sex.*